I WAS ONCE ASHAMED BUT I AM NOW

Forgiven

From Abortion to Healing

Mother and Baby

MARY SULLIVAN

Illustrations by *Mary Sullivan*

WESTBOW
P R E S S®
A DIVISION OF THOMAS NELSON
& ZONDERVAN

WestBow Press books may be ordered through booksellers or by contacting:

WestBow Press
A Division of Thomas Nelson & Zondervan
1663 Liberty Drive
Bloomington, IN 47403
www.westbowpress.com
1 (866) 928-1240

ISBN: 978-1-9736-1884-3 (sc)
ISBN: 978-1-9736-1885-0 (e)

Library of Congress Control Number: 2018901465

Print information available on the last page.

WestBow Press rev. date: 02/05/2018

To those who are contemplating having an abortion or have gone through an abortion. May you find some strength, help, and hope in these pages.

CONTENTS

INTRODUCTION

This story is written about the choices I made, the things I went through, and the secrets I kept for so many years—from being sexually molested and abused as a child, to getting married as a teenager and what led me to having an abortion. You will read how God has brought me through those times and showed me how to deal with them and how to heal. Now I feel led to share my story in hopes of helping others.

ACKNOWLEDGMENTS

I want to thank those who helped me as I unraveled this dark place in my past and opened my heart to share it with others. First, I would like to thank God for His mercy, grace, forgiveness, and love. I would like to thank my husband, Jack Sullivan, for being such a wonderful support through all the hours I put into this book and for being there when I needed a shoulder to cry on. I also want to thank my children, Mitch and Castilia, for encouraging me to write this book and being there when I asked them for their advice. I love each one of you and thank you for who you are in my life.

1

Family Ties

As a child, my family life included both my mother and father, three brothers, and five sisters. One of my sisters died when she was just a few hours old, so while I was growing up, there were actually eight of us siblings living with our parents. All of my siblings, including me, were born in Massachusetts, except for my brother Fred, who was born in North Carolina. I am a twin, and we are second from the youngest. My parents named me Mary, and they named my twin sister Martha after the Mary and Martha in the Bible. It seems funny since Martha seems to worry more and I am more at ease with things, just like in the Bible. We are very close though. We are fraternal and not identical twins, although I seem to know or feel when something is wrong with Martha or when she is feeling down, etc. There is a fifteen-year span between my oldest and youngest brother.

My dad always had a job, and my mother stayed home and took care of all of us children and the household. I never saw either one of my parents complain about their responsibilities as parents, nor did I see or hear them argue or fight. I thought this was normal, that all married couples got along and never fought or argued. My parents never talked about financial issues in front of us kids either. They felt that financial issues were only for adults to worry about and not us children. Some people might say that we lived a very sheltered life. We just didn't know any different. We went to church every Sunday, Wednesday nights, and sometimes on an occasional Friday night. Sometimes they would teach Sunday school or my dad would lead the song service. There were so many kids in our family that we took up the whole bench when we attended a church service. Sometimes my parents would invite other families to our house for different occasions. The adults would socialize or have a Bible study while us kids were off playing in another room.

My parents even had a couple of foster children live in our home for a short time. I also remember my parents caring for a man who was paralyzed from the waist down and was in an electric wheelchair. He loved to give us kids a ride on his lap, and we would push the little toggle switch to go forward or reverse. I remember that it was a lot of fun for both us and him. He seemed to be a very nice man and was very friendly and kind. He also lived with us for a short time. Sometimes our parents (I think it was more my father than my mother) would invite a homeless person into our home for a meal. I believe they wanted to teach us that even though we weren't rich, there were always others out there who were worse off than we were.

I remember one time when they invited an alcoholic man to eat dinner with us. I believe it was on a Sunday, after church. On that day, the man asked to use our bathroom and was in there for the longest time. My father went to check on him and realized that he had gotten into the bathroom cabinet and drank my father's aftershave because it had alcohol in it. My parents didn't get mad at him. They just talked to him about how his life could change with God's help. There were other times during our travels when my father would stop on the side of the road to help someone with a broken-down car. Both of my parents were very caring people, and they taught us to be caring as well.

Our family always seemed to have food on the table and clothes to wear. It always amazed me that we never had a garden to help with the food for our large family. I guess that was because we moved so many times. My siblings and I never knew the reasons why we moved so much and still don't know to this day. Dad was in the navy when he and my mother met. He fought in World War II, but after the war, he got out of the service. He was in the service when my oldest brother and sister were just babies, so it wasn't because of his service that we moved so much. It was almost every year that we would move from the East Coast of the United States to the West Coast. We lived in Massachusetts, California, Virginia, North Carolina, and Washington State.

We were always clean and well dressed, even though I don't remember going to a store to buy new clothes except one time when I was a child. Most of the time we had hand-me-downs from someone in the family, friends, or people from church. We liked going to yard sales or the Goodwill. I don't ever remember wearing ragged or torn clothes. Our mother always made sure we looked nice. I can truly say we were well-mannered kids and knew better than to talk back or complain. When we got out of line, my dad always did the spanking, and yes, if we were really bad, we would get the belt across our bottom or soap in our mouths. We were taught to respect our parents and other adults, to never talk back, to do as we were told, and to not to ask the reason why. This was good in some ways because we showed respect to adults, but I believe it also caused some confusing issues with my trust in authority figures.

Each time we moved Dad had a job lined up, but it was so hard starting all over again in a new neighborhood, going to new schools, and making new friends. It got to the point I really didn't even care about making true friends because I knew we would move and not ever see them again. I would be friendly and play with other kids, but I felt like there was no need to really get to know them. I attended school in the mid-1960s and 1970s. In those days, we didn't have the internet or cell phones to keep in contact with our friends or relatives, and long-distance phone calls cost a lot of money.

Our relatives on my dad's side of the family lived in Massachusetts, and our relatives on my mother's side of the family lived in either North Carolina or Virginia. My grandfather on my father's side died before I was born, and my grandmother (whom we called *Me'me'* which was French for grandmother) I didn't get to know very well or not for very long because of our moves. She could speak fluent French, and she spoke it very fast. I do remember at one place we lived in Massachusetts, she came to live with us for a couple of months because she had fallen and broken her arm. It was the first time I really got to know her. I remember her showing me how to crochet. She seemed very patient. She was a very strong Catholic, and I remember her kneeling down to pray by her bed at night. She would hang her rosary above her bed. I enjoyed having her there. I remember she was very active. She loved to go for walks. I believed she lived until she was eighty-seven years old.

As for my grandparents on my mother's side, the only

memory I have of my grandmother (Granny Ida) was being told that she was my step-grandmother (because my biological grandmother died from complications giving birth to my mother). Granny Ida was very ill and was bedridden. She had some physical and mental issues. My grandfather we called Grandpop. He lived in North Carolina, so we only saw him when we would move from the East Coast to the West Coast, usually in the summer time for a day or two. He seemed nice, but I never got to know him. I was sad about that. The last time I saw any of my grandparents I was around eleven years old.

As we got older and my older brothers and sisters got married or went into the service, some of them lived on the East Coast of the United States, and some lived on the West Coast. On the upside to all the moving, we were able to see most of the United States as we always traveled by car, pulling a trailer or U-Haul behind us. I remember during some of our travels, we were able to see the White House, the Statue of Liberty, the Wright Brothers' monument, the Grand Canyon, the Atlantic Ocean, the Pacific Ocean, various landscapes, and different cultures. To me, it was exciting and interesting. I wish I would have paid a little more attention back then, but as a kid, the sites were neat to see but I didn't know much about the history of any of them or didn't seem to care.

By the time I was seven years old, my oldest brother, Norm, went into the service, and my oldest sister, Margie, got married. Within the next couple of years, my brother, Fred, who is about nine years older than I, went into the marines. Approximately a year after that, one of my other sisters, Estelle, got married, which left four of us kids at home (Regina, Martha, Phil, and me). Because the year span between all of us were so far apart, it was like I really didn't know my older brothers and sisters very much. Margie used to help our mother around the house with the chores, meals, and taking care of us younger kids. As my older siblings left home and got married, I would visit them at their homes. By this time, they had children, and I was an aunt, which I loved. Martha and I would babysit them. I really didn't get to know my older siblings until I reached my thirties and early forties. They were busy starting their own families, and we were always traveling, moving from one place to another.

2

Secrets of Abuse

Just about a year or so before I turned thirteen, I started to be sexually abused. This went on for a few years. It took many years before I felt like I could open up and talk to anyone about this. I felt so confused, lost, damaged, and helpless. Thank God I am free of being a victim and have worked through those issues. Being molested and abused has made me grow into who I am today. The abuse came from a family member I trusted and thought I could look up to.

As a child

Because he was a family member, I felt like I couldn't say anything to anyone. I had to go on like nothing ever happened. I remember after it happened to me, a couple of times I asked my sister to go with me into the bathroom at our house. I told her that I needed to talk to her and that I had a secret to tell her. When it came right down to telling her what was going on, I froze. I couldn't tell her, so I came up with something else to talk about and put the incidents in the back of my mind once again. I felt like I couldn't let anyone know what was going on.

There were so many thoughts that ran through my head, so many questions like: *Is it my fault? Did I do something to provoke this? Why did he choose me? Did he do this to other children or any of my sisters? Was I singled out, and if so, then why me? If I were to tell someone, anyone, about this, what would they think of me? Would they believe me? How would it affect others, especially since it is a close family member?* I was so worried about it causing problems within our family that I just felt like I couldn't tell anyone.

To this day I remember the house we lived in the first time I was molested. I am amazed that I remember this house after all the places we lived. It is a very vivid memory. It was a two-bedroom house in California. One bedroom was for us three girls (Regina, Martha, and me). The other bedroom was our parents' bedroom, which had their bed in there, along with a small bed (actually a cot) for my little brother (Phil) to sleep on. I can still picture the bedroom in which it happened and when the man who molested me came in. I was in bed taking a nap. He laid with me and slowly started touching me and asking me to touch him. I wondered where everyone else was. No one else seemed to be home.

I can still remember him doing things to me. He told me that I had to keep it a secret and that it was only between him and me. He tried to reassure me a few times that it wasn't a bad thing he was doing, but I knew it was. He also tried telling me that it was a normal thing that people do and not to be afraid. I just knew I didn't want to be there. I wished I could just get up and leave, but I couldn't. I was the child, and he was the adult. I was so scared. I remember I actually felt petrified and didn't know what to do. Afterward I pretended to go to sleep. I still don't remember what happened after that. I can't remember if he got up and left, if I got up, or if anyone came home. The rest of that day is a blank to me.

As I looked around my world, I wondered how many other kids had been molested or affected in a similar way. How many of them wanted to speak out, just like me, and tell their story? And how many kept silent just like me? Should I keep silent, or should I tell someone? Maybe if I told someone, it would stop. Was this a normal thing adults did to children? Was I to submit to this person since he was my elder? After all, that's what I had always been taught to do. I knew what was happening to me was wrong, but I just didn't know what to do about it or who to turn to.

While I was growing up, I don't remember hearing about children being abused or molested. People are more open to talk about it now. Today we hear of teachers, leaders, family members, church members, and so forth., who are molesters or predators. People in these positions are the ones children seem to trust the most. I truly believe it happened as much back then as it does now, only it wasn't an open subject. Now it's on the TV, in the newspapers, on the internet, or even talked about at schools.

There were still so many thoughts and questions that ran through my head, even as a child. I was so confused, stressed, and worried. I just didn't know how to process what was going on in my life or what to do about it. I felt I had no right to question what was going on. I knew it was wrong, but I was just a kid. I tried to stay away from the situation and this person as much as I could. Those were the moments when I just wanted to scream. I wanted to let my voice be heard. I wanted the memories to disappear. I just couldn't believe it was happening to me. *Why me anyway? What did I do to deserve this? What could I do to make it stop?* I wanted to tell the world, and yet I wanted to hide and cry and never be seen again.

What I have learned is that no matter what anyone else says or does to you, and no matter what you are going through, you have a mind and a will that God gave you to do what you feel is right in God's eyes and in yours. Don't be silent. Talk with someone. Tell a good friend or a member of your family, or maybe even a counselor, but make sure that this person you talk with is someone you can trust. At least by talking about it you can get some answers or some direction of who to talk to or where to go for help.

I kept silent for years until I was in my twenties. By this time, I was married and had children of my own. The memories of the abuse came back so strong when I saw my daughter grow to the age I was when I was abused. It brought back so many vivid memories. I had nightmares and flashbacks. It seemed strange because I thought I had put it so far back in my mind that I wouldn't have to face it ever again. But that wasn't the case. It was like I was reliving it all over again.

I finally spoke with a counselor when I was in my late twenties. I wasn't sure I wanted to talk with a stranger because, in my mind, I felt that talking wouldn't make things any better or easier, and of course it wouldn't make it go away. It did help somewhat to deal with things and sort them out. But I also knew it was something I had to deal with deep inside.

Before I even went to see the counselor, I decided that I needed to confront my abuser face-to-face, and I did just that. Prior to seeing him, I had asked Martha if he had ever touched her in any way. She admitted to me that he had fondled her breast one time when she was around twelve or thirteen. She said she just pretended she was asleep through the whole thing. Thank God, he didn't touch her after that. Before confronting him, I prayed that God would give me the strength to say what I needed to say to him. It was so very hard to do, but it was a huge stepping stone that I needed to conquer to go on with my life and to heal emotionally. I did not go alone when I confronted him. Martha came to support me, and of course the Holy Spirit was there to guide me. I also confronted him with his wife present.

I had many years of built-up fear, anger, and frustration, but I asked God to help me with just the right words to say. I let him know that I could forgive him because Christ had forgiven me of my sins. Although, I told him I could never forget what happened and that I knew I couldn't trust him alone with my children or my grandchildren. His wife seemed shocked and angry and asked many questions. To my surprise, he didn't deny any of it. He said it was long ago and that he didn't think it would really affect me that much. He thought I would have just forgotten it even happened, like it was no big deal. I don't remember getting an apology from him, but I felt better knowing I exposed him and let him know that I didn't forget. I wanted him to know how it affected me as a child and as an adult and how it stayed with me all those years. It also helped me knowing that I was on my way to recovery.

3

Married Young

While I was in my early teens, the summer before I started high school, we moved to a very peaceful little town in Washington. It was such a big adjustment from the schools down in California. We went from attending a large school to attending a very small one with fewer than thirty kids in our whole freshman class. I welcomed the change. Everyone seemed to know everyone. There were no gangs or crimes like there were down in California. That is where I met my boyfriend, Mike, who later became my husband. We actually planned to get married a few years after we graduated, but things didn't work out that way.

Part of the reason we married so young was that my parents decided our family was going to move again at the end of my junior year of high school, and Mike and I didn't want to be split apart again. This time my family would move from Washington State to California. Just in my freshman, sophomore, and junior years of high school, we moved seven times. This included moving out of state a couple of times, then back to the small town, and then to two different cities close by, all while transferring schools each time.

During the beginning of our junior year of high school, we moved from our small town to the city about thirty miles away. Martha and I decided that we would drive every day to our small-town school so we could still attend our junior year there. We lived out of the school district, but we didn't care. We thought that after all, we had actually gone to this school for two years (on and off). This was the longest time we had ever gone to one school in our lives. We wanted to graduate there with our friends. We wanted to still be part of our class, so we did just that. We'd get up early in the morning and drive to school and then drive the thirty minutes back home again after school. We were happy to still be going to school with our friends. Then came the summer between our junior and senior year of school. Mom and Dad were talking about moving back to California again! Our parents never discussed why we needed to move, just that we were moving.

Mike and I discussed whether he should move to California with my family so we could be still be together, but that was not an option for us. We both wanted to be able to graduate with our class. We knew we planned on getting married someday anyway, so we decided—why not now? We came up with a plan and decided we would do just that. At least that way we wouldn't be torn apart. We could finish our senior year and graduate from high school together. So Mike asked my father for my hand in marriage. My father said yes, but he told Mike that he had to prove how he was going to care for me. He and I both worked at a cafe after school. He was a cook, and I was a waitress. My parents wanted to make sure he could support me. They were both taught that the man had to care for the woman. My parents approved of us getting married, so we set a date for the wedding in July in the summer between our junior and senior year of high school.

Martha also was married in August of that same year.

Martha and I previously had plans to graduate from high school and get a little apartment together before we would get married, but as you see, that didn't work out. Martha was pregnant when she got married. She married the father of her child, who was sixteen years old at the time. She was seventeen. They were not able to finish school. It was a real struggle for them, but her husband was able to get a job as a mechanic at a car dealership.

Mike was eighteen and I was seventeen when we got married. We went to our senior year of school together while we were married and worked part-time jobs. Things seemed to be going well. We had a car and a cute little one-bedroom house that we rented. We were proud of ourselves for trying to finish school and work at the same time to support ourselves. We dreamed of someday having a family and owning our own home, just as most people did. Don't get me wrong—there were a lot of struggles we went through just trying to make ends meet. But we worked hard and didn't depend on anyone else to make it through. I remember one time we were between paychecks and didn't have much food in the house, so we went up in the mountains close by our house and shot a squirrel. We had a single potato in our kitchen, so we made squirrel and a baked potato for our dinner. We didn't want to tell anyone, especially our parents, that we were struggling. But I can say those times made us appreciate what we did have.

We later finished our schooling, got full-time jobs, and moved to a bigger place. We tried to get pregnant for a couple of years but weren't able to for some reason. We went to different doctors and had tests done to find out why we couldn't conceive. There seemed to be no medical explanation.

We were sad that we were not able to conceive, but we were still happy with our lives together. Things seemed to be going well, so we put an offer in on a house to buy. We were so excited. We decided not to worry about getting pregnant until we got settled into our new place and got on our feet again.

I then became sick, constantly having a cold and a sore throat and just not feeling well. I finally went to see a specialist at an eye and ear clinic and found out that I needed to have my tonsils removed. The day I was scheduled for the tonsillectomy, my doctor asked me if I thought I could be pregnant. I told him I didn't think so, but I hadn't had my period for a couple of months. That was nothing new for me because my periods were never on time, so I really wasn't concerned. My doctor decided he wanted to do an exam before the surgery to make sure I wasn't pregnant. Well, guess what? I was pregnant! What a surprise.

4

To Our Surprise

I called Mike and told him not to meet me at the hospital as planned and that the tonsillectomy had been canceled. Then I asked him to meet at home because there was something I needed to share with him. I could hardly wait for him to get home. When I told him, he was as excited as I was. Of course, that meant I would not be getting my tonsils out for a while. We still ended up buying the house we put the offer on. We were excited to be able to decorate one of the bedrooms as a nursery. I did have some morning sickness during my pregnancy, but all in all I felt pretty good. I even worked up until the very end of my pregnancy when our son was born. We named him Mitch, and he had dark-blond hair and blue eyes.

I remember how proud we were when Mitch was born. What a blessing from God! He was such a good baby. I definitely didn't want to go back to work. Mike and I both wanted me to be able to stay home with Mitch, but we couldn't afford that. One paycheck just wasn't enough to pay the bills, so back to work I went. I remember leaving Mitch with the babysitter for the first time when he wasn't quite two months old.

We didn't put him in a regular daycare because we felt

like he would get more attention from a woman we knew personally. Her name was Gloria. She and her husband had a child of their own. Gloria was a great person with a gentle spirit. Part of me felt comfortable leaving him with her because I knew he would be safe, and yet part of me felt like a piece of my heart was being ripped away when I left him there. The first day I left him, I walked out of their house and slowly got into my car, looking back as I walked away. I backed out of her driveway and headed to work with tears in my eyes. I couldn't wait for the workday to end. It seemed like it went by so slowly. Each day that I left him at the babysitter's house, it didn't get any easier, but I knew I had to do it.

A couple of months had gone by since Mitch was born, and my tonsils had gotten worse. The doctor told me they needed to come out, so I took a few days off work and went in and had the tonsillectomy. Life seemed to be going by so fast. After I returned back to work for about a month after my tonsillectomy, I started feeling sick to my stomach. I just couldn't keep anything down. It felt like morning sickness all over again. I mentioned to Mike that I felt like I was pregnant again, but he said, "There is just no way you can be pregnant. We've been really careful, and we used protection." I told him I had those same thoughts but my body was telling me something totally different.

Well about eight months later, we had our second child, a little baby girl. We named her Castilia after my mother. We felt our family was complete. It was perfect—a little boy first and now a little girl. Castilia had dark hair and blue eyes. She was beautiful. (She still is to this day, inside and out.) She was a miracle baby because while I was pregnant with her, my body kept trying to miscarry her due to the fact that I had gotten pregnant so soon after having our son, and my body still hadn't recovered from the tonsillectomy. I had to stay in bed throughout most of my pregnancy. Needless to say, I had to quit my job. My mother came over quite often to help me with Mitch since I couldn't be up on my feet very long at a time. Each time I got up, I would have contractions, and I still had months to go before delivery.

Mitch was born on June 8 of one year, and our Castilia was born the following year on June 6. I actually came home from the hospital with Castilia on Mitch's first birthday. Martha threw a little birthday party for Mitch and a welcome home party from the hospital for Castilia and me at the same time. It was a beautiful day. Both set of grandparents showed up, along with some other family and friends. Martha had made a chocolate cake with chocolate frosting and gave Mitch his first slice of birthday cake. What a mess he was. I remember him sitting in the high chair all covered with chocolate—chocolate all in his hair, on his face, on his ears. He thoroughly enjoyed every bite.

After several discussions and some financial planning, Mike and I decided it would be best for me to stay home and take care of our children. He was working as a mechanic for a company that repaired and made fruit-packing equipment. It would be hard, but we decided we would make things work out financially with only his paychecks. It was just impossible to try to pay for daycare for the two babies if I worked also. It seemed to work out well for a while. I know I was happy to stay home and take care of our children. Mike started looking for a higher-paying mechanic job to make ends meet. Keep in mind we were just twenty-two and twenty-three years old at that time.

About a year went by when Mike was offered a job in Seattle. It was only a few hours from the rest of our family. It was a higher-paying job and a great opportunity for him. He was excited about it, and we believed we would finally be able to get ahead financially. He accepted the job, and we made the move toward the new adventure in our lives. The children were just one and two years old at the time. Because we couldn't afford the high cost of renting in Seattle, we had to live about twenty miles away, so Mike had to commute to work each day. It was about a half hour to an hour of driving each way depending on the traffic. People used to ask us how we were always so happy together. We went to school together and even worked together for a few years.

5

Where Is God?

During those years, I had drifted away from church and God. Mike was never one to go to church with me. He always believed that God was in his heart and he didn't need to go to a church to worship Him. He went to church with me when we dated but quit going after we got married. He loved to be outside and in the mountains and believed that was a great place to worship. I was raised in church and was taught and believed that I needed to go to church. I slowly drifted away after I got married and then quit going to church altogether.

I believe with all my heart that God is in your heart and not in a building. But I also believe God wants us to go to church. (This gathering place could be in a building or in someone's home. It could be just about anywhere. It's about people who worship God and listens to His word.) By gathering like this, it gives us accountability as we are only human. Even the Bible tells us that if two or three are gathered in His name, there He will be also. We are sinners who are justified through the blood of Jesus, but we are still growing in Christ Jesus to be more like Him. My life was sure different without Him in it, but I couldn't see it then or didn't want to admit it.

Life seemed to get harder as the children grew and money got tighter. We had imagined that this would be a great time in our lives and that it would also be a great opportunity to get caught up on our bills and get ahead in life. It would also be a great opportunity for Mike to get the training he had been looking for with this new job. But to my surprise, it seemed that once we moved to the Seattle area, the alcohol, the troubles, and the lonely days and nights began. It seemed that Mike was never home to share the gifts that God had given us—our children, Mitch and Castilia, who were just one and two years old at the time. Mike and I had gotten along great throughout the first five and a half years of our marriage until it seemed that alcohol took over. I felt like Mike started drinking because it was his way of coping with the responsibilities of taking care of a wife and two children. I didn't have any idea that alcoholism ran so deeply in his family (his biological family, that is) or I guess I never really knew how difficult it was to pull away from alcoholism. He had been adopted as a young child and never realized how vulnerable to alcohol he was. As for me, I don't ever remember seeing any alcohol in our home or being anywhere around us when I was a child, so as I became an adult, seeing the effects of alcohol was totally new to me.

I do remember that in one of our moves across the country while we were down in California, we stopped at my mother's cousin Hilda's house. She was married to a man named James. The first day we were there, our parents were inside the house talking with Hilda and James. All of us kids were in a camper my dad had built, which was on the back of his truck. The truck was parked on the road next to the sidewalk in front of Hilda and James's house. It was a beautiful day, the sun was out, and we were enjoying just being kids. We were out in the camper talking and noticed that when we looked out the window once in a while, we would see James come out of his house and look around like as if to make sure no one was watching him. He had no idea we were watching behind the curtain in the camper. He would then walk over to the bushes in front of their house and pull out a bottle from within the bushes. He would then take a drink, look around again, and then put the bottle back in the bushes

At first we had no idea what he was doing until we figured it out, and being kids, we decided that we wanted to play a trick on him. One time when he went inside the house, we ran over to the bushes, got his bottle (of whiskey), and poured the rest of it out in the grass. We then filled the bottle with water. We were so careful not to let him see what we were doing. After a bit, James came out of the house again and went looking for his bottle in the bushes. Again he looked around to make sure no one was watching him. He took a swig of it and spit it out. He was not a very happy man! He started cussing and looking around, trying to figure out who did this to him. At first we thought it was funny. We were laughing behind the curtain in the camper. As we saw him and heard him, I started to feel bad for him. He looked angry and confused. He went in the house. He came out and looked around again and then went back inside.

Within a few minutes, our parents came out to the camper and asked us if we knew what was going on. We then told them what we did. They explained that James had an addiction to alcohol, and it was not right what we had done to him. Needless to say, we had to apologize to him. I don't remember what happened after that. I do remember he was upset with us though. Now that I know about addiction and how it affects people, I realize we not only dumped his whiskey out but we upset his world in those moments. It is sad to me that he actually lived his life this way.

6

Becoming Strangers

Mike started his drinking innocently enough by just having a few beers with the guys or friends when they would come over for a barbeque or a dinner or sometimes just to visit. To us it was just part of people socializing. I would have never thought that it would or could take over his life like it did. Don't get me wrong—I would have a glass of wine when we had friends over, but I'd sip on one glass all night long. I didn't really care for the taste of alcohol, and I especially didn't like being out of control in any way. I couldn't understand how anyone could get to the point of not being able to say no to another drink or just walk away from it. It took me a few years to find out that it isn't that easy for some people. I feel I am really blessed and thankful that alcoholism doesn't run in my veins.

When we moved to the Seattle area into an apartment complex, two of Mike's coworkers lived in the same apartment complex with their wives and children. All of our apartments were close and within walking distance from each other. I thought that was great because I didn't know anyone when we first moved there. I looked forward to getting to know the wives of Mike's coworkers and their children. I thought it would be nice to have them to hang out with during the day, especially since they all had children as well. Well I found out that these couples loved to party a lot. I am a very social person and I liked to party, but not this kind of partying. There was a lot of hard liquor and smoking pot, along with taking speed or as it was called back then "black beauties."

The men (including Mike) never came home until late at night. One of the wives was cheating on her husband with some guy who lived in another apartment in the complex. She would actually sneak out of her apartment at night while her husband was sleeping to be with this other guy. The other coworker's wife was not only taking drugs, but she was selling them. The children suffered for sure! It was really sad. This lifestyle was really different and difficult for me. I felt out of place. I badly wanted to move back to our small hometown, but I thought we should at least give this a try. Maybe things would settle down in time.

Because of the distance to Mike's work, and since we only had one car, most of the time he would take the car to work. Once in a while, if I needed the car to get groceries or go to appointments, I would get the children ready early in the morning and drive him to work. It took a lot of gas (which we couldn't afford) and time, so I didn't do this very often. I felt all alone at times. I kept telling myself this was supposed to be helping us get ahead, but it didn't. We were getting further behind financially and drifting further apart physically, mentally, and emotionally. The burden of the finances and being in a new environment along with peer pressure affected both of us, but I knew it affected Mike even more. At this point his drink of choice was whiskey.

Whiskey Bottle

He and the other mechanics would drink at work. They had their own shop area where no one else was allowed. This was where they would gather to drink whiskey and smoke pot. This is where Mike's addiction to whiskey began.

There were days when I would make dinner, waiting for him to come home from work, but he wouldn't come home for hours. He clocked out of work but didn't come straight home. They would stop at the bars. Sometimes he didn't get home for four or five hours after leaving work. When he did arrive home, the dinner that I had prepared was cold and dried out. I'd be upset. He'd be upset as well as drunk most the time. He would tell me that he had to stop at the bar with the guys until the traffic died down. We would get into arguments until we just didn't care to talk to each other anymore. I was thankful he didn't get in a wreck driving home.

His drinking got to be a normal, everyday thing in our lives. We talked about it and fought about it time after time, until one day I said that I was taking the kids and moving back to our hometown and that he needed to decide if he was going to move back with us or if he was staying. After long discussions, he decided that we would move back as a family. I was happy that we were going to get away from the environment we were in, and I figured that life would get back to normal again. I had no idea that it wouldn't be that easy.

We moved back to the small town, and Mike got a job at a warehouse as a mechanic. He built things, repaired things, and even invented machinery for the company. However, he still had a drinking problem. He hid it from people very well. He knew it had control over him. He thought that maybe if he tried drinking beer instead of whiskey that might help him, but it didn't. He even tried drinking nonalcoholic beer. That didn't work either. He tried to quit drinking altogether, but he just couldn't let go. (Actually it wouldn't let go of him.) So he went back to drinking whiskey. Neither one of us knew where to look for help.

Beer bottle

I believe at this time I became an enabler instead of a help to him. I remember so many times I would cover for his alcoholism, his absenteeism, and his mannerisms. After years of this going on, I felt there was no end in sight. The children weren't quite three and four years old yet. Financially, we were getting nowhere except in trouble. At one point, we were three months behind on rent with an eviction notice (this happened a few times, but each time we would get caught up on rent until it would happen again). Our utility bills were past due. We were so far in debt. We didn't have enough money to live on. Yet there were times when Mike would give money to people who were practically strangers because he felt like they needed it more than we did. He would give his shirt off his back to help someone. He was a very caring person, but he didn't seem to know where his responsibilities should have been—or maybe, because of the alcohol, his reasoning was clouded.

It is a very sad thing when someone gets caught up in any kind of an addiction. It is a hard thing to live with for both the person with the addiction and his or her family members. Everyone involved suffers in some way.

After a while, we started avoiding each other. When he wasn't drinking, it was like being with a whole different person, and he was great to be around. I used to tell myself that someday he would stop drinking and things would change. But he kept drinking, and we kept drifting further and further apart. I didn't care to even be around him the last couple of years of our marriage because of the smell and my disgust of the alcohol. We were living two separate lives under one roof. He went his way, and I went mine. Each day was a new experience. Those experiences were not as husband and wife but as strangers. Our children didn't really know who Daddy was because they didn't see much of him, or when they did see him, he was loud and obnoxious or sleeping or passed out.

The children started having physical problems due to the stress in our household, and I knew they were emotionally being affected as well. Mitch was having problems with his speech. He seemed to stutter a lot. I was taking him to a speech therapist a few times a week. Castilia was potty trained at the time but then all of a sudden started wetting her pants, and it seemed like it was quite often. She just couldn't control it. We found out she had a urinary tract infection, which the doctor felt was due to stress.

It seemed like when Mike was home, he was drinking, and he was in his own world. He knew he had a problem. I knew he had a problem, but I didn't know what to do about it. I knew he loved his children very much, but he just couldn't control himself because of the alcohol. Mike seemed to be tougher on Mitch because he was a boy. He always told Mitch he wasn't supposed to cry because boys don't cry and that he expected more from him because he was a boy. On the other hand, he would let Castilia do just about anything because she was his baby girl and it was cute. He loved both Mitch and Castilia very much and liked to brag about them. He liked to wrestle with Mitch, but sometimes he would get a little too rough with Mitch when he was drinking, so I would have to intervene.

7

Covering up Lies

Little by little Mike wasn't just drinking whiskey but whatever else he could afford, even cheap wine. I would find bottles all over the house, under the couch, in the bathroom cabinet, in the closets, behind the seats of his truck, in his toolbox, and elsewhere. He enjoyed drinking straight whiskey. This made it very difficult to want to be around him or even talk with him because he would forget our conversation from one day to the next or he would repeat himself. I didn't want to go anywhere with him. It was embarrassing for me as well as for him. I believe he actually didn't know what he was saying or doing most of the time. At least, he never seemed to remember anything the next day. It was actually pretty sad because I knew there was a different person inside all that mess.

People would come over to visit and ask where he was. I would say, "Oh, he's taking a nap or resting." I always seemed to cover up the fact that he was drunk and passed out. I guess I felt if I didn't talk about it then no one would know the real reason. That way I wouldn't have to answer a bunch of questions. It was much easier telling them he was asleep. I felt that I had to cover up something that I was going through every day. Now, when I look back at it, I realize I wasn't helping the situation at all. I was just covering it up. I was enabling him by not facing up to the problem. I realized some of this after attending a few meetings at Al-Anon (a meeting place for families of alcoholics). I was able to get Mike to go to one of these meetings. We talked about him going to Alcoholics Anonymous, but he wasn't interested. It did seem to help me some, but I also felt I was at a dead end since he was not interested in going.

Other things began to happen. Several times I would receive phone calls with no voice on the other end of the line. Either the person would hang up when I answered the phone or the person would be silent. When it first started happening, I never thought much about it. I guess I was naïve. Then the hang-up calls got to be more frequent. At that time, I started questioning in my mind but didn't want to believe anything was going on between Mike and any other woman.

Phone on wall

I would think to myself, *This is my life—my husband and our children. There is no way we can have these kinds of problems, not in our marriage.* I would tell myself, *It will all work out. I know it will, if I just work at it hard enough.* I would remind myself that we were married for life—for better or for worse.

Again, I reflected back to my upbringing and my childhood. As I mentioned earlier, I had never been around an alcoholic before. I knew people drank alcohol, but I never realized how much damage it could do to a person or a family. I had no idea how to stop this. I remembered our vows though—that I was married until death do us part. I felt that I loved him so much that I would do just about anything to keep our marriage together. We made those vows, and we were going to keep them (so I thought). Neither one of us had ever dealt with addiction before. Mike was only five when he was taken away from his biological family, so growing up he never put alcohol and addiction together. He remembered his biological parents drinking all the time but didn't think it would ever affect him. But at this point, he realized that he just couldn't control the cravings. He would say he was going to quit but never did. He couldn't. It wasn't that easy. It was a sickness he couldn't control. He was a victim to this awful disease called alcoholism. We started to attend AA (Alcoholic Anonymous) and Al-Anon meetings together. I knew we needed more. Nothing seemed to work.

Both of Mike's biological parents were alcoholics. He had been adopted when he was a child after being in several foster homes. His adoptive parents (Don and Betty) were wonderful people who loved him very much. They were foster parents for so many years to so many children. They also adopted a few of the children to give them a permanent home. The first few years of Mike and my marriage, we searched and searched for his biological parents and found them. Then we went on to find his biological siblings. It took a lot of work and research, but it all worked out in the end. What a great reunion it was, especially when we found his grandmother (Rita). She was such a sweet woman. The reason that he and his siblings were taken away from their biological parents was due to alcohol and the lifestyle that went along with it. Mike has five biological siblings.

Even though he was very young at the time, he remembered what his life was like with his biological parents. He remembered his mother coming home with other men, along with the physical abuse to him and his siblings. He remembered all the parties and the alcohol. He even remembered when the authorities came and took him and his siblings away. He was the oldest child, and he felt it was his fault that they were all taken away. He felt, even as a child, that he wasn't there to protect his brothers and sisters. It was a terrifying time in his life. It affected him tremendously. I remember asking him to talk with a counselor or someone about his past, but he was very strong-willed and believed he could do it all on his own. I believe it would have helped him tremendously to sort things out about his past. Sometimes during our talks, I would remind him of his biological parents' alcoholism and ask him not to let that happen to us, especially for our children's sake, and not to let our family be torn apart because of alcohol. He agreed and would work harder on quitting his drinking. I decided it might be good for me to go back to work again outside the home. It was hard to find an office job because I had been out of the workforce for a couple of years, so I looked for other positions. Mike told me about an opening at the fruit warehouse he worked at. He was a mechanic there. I applied and got the job. I packed apples and pears and sorted cherries.

While I was at work, I kept hearing rumors of Mike with another woman. This woman also worked at the warehouse. I started keeping my ears and eyes open after that. I knew who she was, but like I said, I was naïve—or maybe deep down I just didn't want to believe it. I tried many different things to try to get him interested in me, thinking that maybe this would get the other woman out of his mind and out of our lives. I even decided I would go out drinking and dancing with him. I knew drinking alcohol was the problem, but I decided at that point that I wouldn't bug him about his drinking anymore. I would dress the way he wanted me to, go where he wanted to go, and just have fun as a couple. I wanted our marriage to work out. I was taught that when you got married, it was "until death do us part." As a woman and a wife, I was to do what I could to stay married, no matter what. I couldn't just let a divorce happen to us. We went on this way for a while, but things weren't any better. I started getting anonymous phone calls at our house again. The person on the other end of the phone would always hang up on me or would not talk to me when I said hello.

Talking on the phone

When I got laid off from my seasonal position from the warehouse, I started a daycare in our home to try to keep us financially afloat. I had a daycare for about a year and then later got a full-time job doing office work. While working the daycare, I took care of three other children along with Mitch and Castilia. One of the little girls went to school part time, so I only took care of her a few hours a day. I had one little boy who was allergic to so many things. It was actually sad. He was even allergic to grass and the sunshine on his skin, so if he went outside with all of us, I had to cover him from head to toe and put medicated lotions on his skin. I felt so bad for him. They all were good kids, and they all got along really well.

The income from the daycare helped with food and other everyday expenses we had. I was happy to find something I could do to help bring income in. During this time, Mike still worked at the warehouse, and he would pick this other woman up and they would ride back and forth to work together. We talked about it and disagreed about it a lot, and he tried to convince me that nothing was happening between the two of them. He said that they were just good friends and that he just needed someone to talk to. I kept telling him, "You can talk to me. I'm your wife." He said that I just didn't understand. She was just a friend and someone to talk to, nothing more than that. This seemed to go on for months. The times he would leave for work would get earlier in the morning, and then he would come home later at night. He said he had extra work to take care of. However, this other woman would just happen to stay later at work also and needed Mike to give her a ride home. I suggested that she get a ride home with someone else, but he told me I was overreacting and not to worry.

The anonymous phone calls kept coming in. I later found out that these phone calls were from someone else, not from the woman at the warehouse. This girl happened to be a lot younger than me and was actually a friend of our neighbor across the street from where we lived. I confronted Mike, but he denied it. I realized then that something was going on, but again, I would deny it. I feel so stupid now when I look back at it all.

Mike decided to go to work with a guy who had just opened up his own upholstery shop. He really seemed to like working with upholstery. He was very good with his hands and very creative. He came up with the idea and designed small furniture for children. Their work consisted of reupholstering furniture and also building new furniture for children. They sold their work to retailers. There didn't seem to be a lot of money to be made as they were renting a building and paying for overhead cost and materials. Mike seemed to work long but very odd hours.

One night I decided to go to their place of business. I arrived there and noticed Mike's truck parked in back of the upholstery shop along with a small vehicle parked next to his truck. I knocked on the door, but there was no answer. I knocked again, but still no answer. I knew he had to be in there, but who was he with? I then banged on the door and called out his name a few times and said I knew he was in there and to open the door. I did this a few times until the door finally opened. Mike was on the other side of the door. I asked what took him so long to answer and that I was worried because he hadn't come home yet and it was late. He said he was tired and fell asleep, but he seemed to be acting strange.

I pushed my way through and walked through the shop to find a bed set up in a room with an eighteen-year-old who was half dressed lying in it. I was fuming! I asked what was going on. She just looked at me and didn't say a word. Mike, on the other hand, was trying to make all kinds of excuses. Part of me wanted to just start hitting her, but instead I lost it and started slapping, hitting, and kicking Mike, along with yelling and crying, "How could you?" I had never felt this way in my life! I felt so betrayed. I felt like a fool. He grabbed my wrist and just held my arms up from hitting him. I don't think I'd ever been so angry and hurt in my life before that time. (I had never hit him in my life before then or after that time. I've always been a very calm and mellow person.) She got dressed and left. I calmed down, we talked some, and then we went home in our separate vehicles. This is when I found out who she was and how he met her at our neighbor's house.

8

Divorce?

At that point, we had been married for eight years. We talked several times about our marriage and making things work, until one day I told him that I couldn't go on this way. I remember we were standing in our living room, and the kids were asleep. I told him that I was hurting and I didn't want to live like that anymore. I knew neither one of us was happy with our lives and our marriage, so I asked Mike if he wanted a divorce, and to my surprise, he said *yes*.

I'm sure my lip dropped. I know my heart sank and tears welled up in my eyes. I really expected him to say no and that we needed to work things out. But he didn't. I kept thinking, *This can't be happening.*

I asked him, "What do you mean? And how can you be so cold?"

He said that we had gotten married so young and we never had the chance to date other people. He felt we should both date others, and we should both see what it would be like to be single and free. Keep in mind we had two children. He said we would still love each other and in time we might get back together but that he wanted to date other women for a while. I felt he loved me but that the alcohol had messed with his reasoning.

I really didn't know what to say. It's hard to explain how I felt at that moment. I was angry. I was sad. I was hurt and confused. I do remember saying to him, "If we get divorced, we're divorced! I can't see us dating and sleeping with other people and staying married or getting back together later. That is not a marriage! I've had enough of living this way."

He said that was fine, and that he was okay with it. I was so … hurt. I felt lost and angry. I really thought that if I brought up the word *divorce*, he would at least think about everything and would want to try and work things out. But it wasn't so. I was really upset. I remember that I tried to do whatever it would take to keep my marriage, but I didn't want to keep going on this way. No matter how much I went along with things, it didn't make things any better. It made things worse.

We decided that we would both stay at the house until he found a place to live and move out on his own. The kids would live with me. At one point he did go and stay with his biological father for a few weeks. We separated. Nothing was ever the same. He went out with other women, and I started going out as well. I'll never forget one day a guy picked me up to take me out to dinner, and Mike just stood there at our front door and said goodbye. It was the strangest thing.

Front door entry

In my heart I really didn't care to go out with this guy. He was a nice guy, good-looking and all. He was actually someone who worked as a contractor at my place of employment. (I was working temporarily in an office position, filing and answering phones at this time.) Yet, in my mind, I thought, *Fine … I'll show Mike. I'll go with this guy, and I will have a good time. Maybe Mike will get jealous. Maybe this will affect him after all.* But to this day, I don't think it bothered him. I went out on that date and tried to make it as pleasant as possible, but it felt very strange to me.

I had lost so much weight because of all the stress in my life. I actually weighed less than a hundred pounds. I had always been a small-framed person, but with the weight loss I looked way too thin. I went to see doctors because I had stomach problems. Every morning when I knew I had to face another day, I would end up in the bathroom sitting on the toilet. I would do this several times a day. If I ate anything at all, it would upset my stomach, and back in the bathroom I would be. That was such a terrible time in my life. I was just a bundle of nerves. The doctor just gave me some medications. One was to help me with my stomach issues, and the other was some valium to calm my nerves. I never did take any valium because I knew I had children to take care of and I was scared of the effects it would have on me. I didn't like taking any kind of medicine, not even aspirin.

I decided to go to a business college and get an accounting and data processing degree so I would be able to financially take care of my children and myself. The jobs I had up until then just didn't pay enough for a single mother with two children, and I knew I definitely didn't want to work in a warehouse packing fruit the rest of my life. It just wasn't what I enjoyed doing, and it was seasonal. I wanted more, so I took a four-year course in an eleven-month period and received my degree. The college was only about five miles from where I lived, so that made it convenient, especially since I didn't have much money for gas. The course was Monday through Friday, eight in the morning until late afternoon, with a lot of homework every night.

I was getting assistance to pay for daycare while I went to school. I received grants and also took out student loans to pay for my schooling. I remember borrowing money to pay for my books that the grants didn't cover. My car during that time was a clunker. It always seemed to have problems or break down. It had been duct taped and wired just about all it could. During that time while I was still attending college, Mike decided to move out. He physically moved out, but he still had most of his things at the house. He moved in with a friend of his for a while. I tried to keep my mind busy. It definitely wasn't easy, but I knew that once I graduated, it would give me the opportunity to get a decent job and take care of my children.

While I was attending college, I would go out once in a while with three or four of my girlfriends. We would go out together to a bar so we could dance. They would introduce me to different people. I wasn't much of a drinker, but I loved to dance. I would order a wine and sip on it all night but mostly go out on the dance floor. One night while we were out, my friend introduced me to the bouncer she had known for a while. She had been trying to set us up for some time. A few weeks later, he met my friends and me for dancing and drinking. He worked late that night, so we talked about getting together after he got off work, which we did. We talked for quite a while. I decided to ask him to go home with me.

When we entered my house, I felt so strange and uncomfortable. There were things in my house that were ours—Mike's and mine and our children's. The kids were spending the night at their grandparents' house that night. There were items on the wall or in the bedroom, things that Mike and I shared throughout our eight years of marriage. It just didn't seem right. The man I was with felt my uneasiness and discomfort. In fact, we talked about it. It didn't seem to bother him at all, so I decided that I wouldn't let it bother me either and that I needed to get over Mike and get on with my life. We talked for a while about our lives, my children, and our jobs. We ended up in the bedroom after that.

I remember feeling very awkward and uneasy. *I should have listened to my heart. But I also wanted to feel loved. I wanted someone to hold me—someone to care about me.* It really didn't matter at that point. I just wanted someone to be there with me. The thing was that Mike and I weren't even legally divorced yet. I told myself, *It is okay. Mike is out of the picture now. I just want to have fun and forget about things.* I felt like I was out for revenge, and yet at the same time I just wanted to be needed and loved again, not by someone else but by Mike. I really tried to enjoy being with this man, but I couldn't. My mind was on everything except being in bed with him. I laid there and pretended to enjoy it, but at the same time I thought to myself, *I am with a stranger, someone I don't love. Actually, I really don't even know much about him.* So many things ran through my head; it really wasn't what my heart desired. There weren't any feelings or love involved. It was such an empty feeling. I wondered to myself, *How do people do this all the time and say they had a great time? I just don't understand. How awkward. How crazy my life is.*

9

Am I Really Pregnant?

That night changed my life. It was the night I got pregnant by a stranger. I knew exactly when it happened. I remember oh so well the feeling of conception and how dirty and ashamed I felt. I just wanted him to leave. When he left that night, I asked him to leave out the back door. My thoughts were that I didn't want my neighbors to think badly of me. Although it really didn't matter what the neighbors thought—I was the one who felt terrible, not them. As he left, he didn't seem to care. It was just a night of fun and pleasure for him. There were no feelings at all. He got what he wanted and left.

A couple of days passed by after that night when Mike showed up from being out of town. We talked and then decided that he would move back in. Most of his things were never really gone anyway—just him. He still wanted a divorce, and he still wanted to see other people. At this point I didn't know what I wanted. We thought it would be more convenient for both of us financially if he moved back in until we got everything with the divorce settled and we both got set up in our own places.

As the days and weeks went by, I kept looking at my stomach and wondering was it just my imagination or was there really this little person inside me? I was a small-framed woman, and I had lost so much weight that I could see and feel this little bump on my once-flat belly.

Flat belly

My thoughts were racing. *What am I going to do now that I'm pregnant? I'm basically a single woman now with two small children. What am I going to tell everyone? Should I just tell them I am pregnant?* I talked to Mike about it. He suggested that I have an abortion. I told him I couldn't and wouldn't do that! *How could he even think that?* He said that I should go to the father of this child and ask for his opinion and let him know that he was the father. I agreed with that. Mike actually suggested that he would go with me, which he did. To my surprise, when I confronted the father, he straight out said to abort "it." To him it wasn't a child, just an inconvenience, and a problem to be fixed. The baby was an "it," as he put it. There wasn't any hesitation from him at all. He didn't want anything to do with it. To him, it was just a one-night fling. Mike looked at me as if to say, "I told you so."

As I left the father, my mind started wondering. *What will this child be like? I love children. What is one more child? I'll be okay with three children.* The more Mike and I talked, the more he was convinced that the abortion was the right thing to do. After all, this child would have a different father and a different name than my other two children. Whether Mike and I worked things out in the future or not, this child was from another man—someone I didn't really even know.

Mike asked me, "What are we going to tell everyone? What will people think?"

I decided to talk with my friend who introduced me to the father of my unborn child. Not letting her know why I was asking these questions, I started asking her, "What kind of a person is he? What is his everyday life like? What is his family like? How long have you known him?"

I wanted as much information as I could; after all, he was the father of my unborn child. She informed me that he was a nice guy. She said that she knew he used drugs once in a while and was a drinker, but all in all, he was a nice guy and fun to be around. She then informed me that the drugs he used were hard drugs and that he had been using them for a while, but again, she thought he was a nice guy. I was upset that she hadn't told me all of this before, but I guess to her it wasn't important. I, of course, didn't want to tell her why I was asking all these questions. She couldn't tell me much more than that because that was all she knew about him. She got acquainted with him through the bar.

I should have asked all these questions in the beginning,

before ever thinking of being with him. And in all actuality, I shouldn't have ever been with anyone. It was kind of too late to be asking any questions at that point. Then all these things started racing in my mind. *Wow … What did I do? I got pregnant by someone I really didn't know at all—someone who uses drugs. I went from one mess and made another. How will it affect the baby since the father took drugs? Will the baby be physically or mentally disabled, or what should I expect? Will it be a drug baby? What will this baby's future be like? Will this child be okay? What should I do?* I didn't know anyone who seriously took any drugs. Now what was I going to do? I was a mess.

Then I thought that maybe Mike and the father of this child were right. I got to thinking maybe I should abort this child. But then I told myself, *I can't do something like this. I just can't!*

I spoke with Mike again, knowing that our marriage was not healthy anyway. It was actually over. We both agreed that we were going to try to make our marriage work again, but he still felt that I should go through with the abortion. This way we wouldn't have any other problems to solve—not that an abortion would solve any problems. As I thought of our marriage or being a single mother of three, I asked myself, *What should I do? Which way should I turn?* I wanted our marriage to work so badly. I asked myself over and over again, *Should I? No, I can't!* But then I made that awful decision to go through with the abortion.

I kept trying to convince myself that Mike was right. I asked myself, *What could be so wrong? People do this every day. After all, this wouldn't even be allowed if it was something that was illegal or wrong. Besides, I am only six weeks along and they say it's not a baby until after twelve weeks.*

In the early '80s the procedure was taken care of in the doctor's office, just like any other procedure. Deep inside I knew it was wrong and that I would regret it, and yet I still went through with it. I really can't tell you why except that I wanted to keep my marriage and I felt like this was what I needed to do. I thought someday I would probably regret it. That was an absolute understatement! That someday was then and now! There will never be a way to turn back time, never! I look back and ask myself, *How could I have forgotten my morals, my upbringing, or my God?*

Mike went with me to the clinic. He stayed in the room with me. As we arrived, I knew I was making a mistake and suggested to him that maybe this wasn't such a good idea. I figured our marriage would be all right with a third child. I loved children, and having one more wouldn't be any different than having two. We could go ahead and have the child and no one would ever know that the baby wasn't his except for the two of us. It would be a lie to cover up what I had done.

Mike reminded me that we already had the appointment and needed to keep it. To this day, I don't remember making the appointment. I'm sure I must have, but I guess my mind has blocked it out. I do remember being in the waiting room; I remember wanting to run out of there. I also remember the doctor talking to the two of us and asking Mike if this is what he wanted also. They actually had him sign a form stating that he also wanted the abortion. After all they just assumed it was his child I was carrying. I remember the doctor's office and the room where the procedure was done. Mike mentioned to me again while we were in the waiting room that the father didn't want anything to do with the child or any responsibility. He felt we were making the right decision. It seemed that the doctors, nurses, and personnel at the clinic regarded it as just another medical procedure that happened every day. And to them, I guess it was. This was not a specialty clinic for abortions. It was our regular clinic that you might go in to see a doctor when you were sick or maybe go in for x-rays, or even see an OB-GYN for a checkup or pregnancy.

10

In the Waiting Room

While sitting and waiting to see the doctor, a nurse came in the waiting room and called my name. My heart sank. Mike and I looked at each other and stood up. She brought us down the hall and into a room. As we entered the room, I saw the equipment that was to be used. I got undressed, put the gown on, and sat on the table. I remember feeling so cold. I was so nervous; I decided that I couldn't go through with it after all. I looked at the door. I was shaking.

Then I heard a knock on the door and then someone say, "Can we come in?"

I just froze. The doctor and nurse came into the room. Mike held my hand. I'm sure he could see the scared and indecisive look on my face. He kept quietly saying, "It will be all right. We talked about this, and this is something we need to do. It's for the best."

The nurse and doctor looked at me and said, "It's not that bad. It will only take a few minutes; you might feel a couple of cramps. It doesn't take long, and you'll be on your way. It will all be over with soon."

Those last words, "It will all be over with soon," cannot begin to tell the story. It wasn't over. The hurt, the pain, and the lies had just begun.

I remember while I was sitting on the table, the nurse asked me to lie down and put my feet up in the stirrups, and of course I heard the words, "Scoot your bottom down to the edge," just as if it was just another pap smear or checkup. They put on their gloves and then asked how I was doing. I couldn't say a word. I just nodded my head. I felt numb inside. My heart was aching. My thoughts were racing. But all I could do was cry inside and hide my feelings. Mike was there, still holding my hand, telling me it was okay and that everything would be fine. He thought he was comforting me by saying we were making the right decision and that we couldn't go on together unless we followed through with this procedure. It just wouldn't be right for anyone involved. He felt that several people would suffer if I didn't go through with it. Those people he was talking about included him, the father of the child, the child inside me, and me. This decision was something we had made together. To be honest with you, I don't think we realized or thought of how it would affect our future as well the future of everyone else involved, including my child's life here on earth. I believe the only thing we thought of at the time was the immediate future and nothing really much further than that.

Doctor's office

While I laid there on the table, I kept thinking to myself, *I can still leave, if I leave right now.* I kept closing and opening my eyes, looking around the room, thinking, *What am I doing here?* The nurse started preparing the instruments on the tray by where I was laying. I remember staring at those instruments, not knowing what was going to happen next. Then they brought in a big piece of equipment, a machine I called a vacuum.

They gave me a shot, and the doctor told me that there was no turning back; we had to follow through with the procedure. The shot would start the abortion process. My heart felt numb. My throat felt like a hard lump was in it. I couldn't speak. I closed my eyes and cried within. I could hear the metal table being wheeled around me, the instruments vibrating on the table with every wheel that turned. I could hear the doctor and nurse talking and passing things back and forth. I don't even remember what they said. My mind was only on the procedure and what was being done. I then felt the pain as the instruments entered my body. It felt like very strong and painful menstrual cramps without easing up. *This pain was nothing compared to the pain I felt inside knowing what I was doing.* I could hear a noise that sounded like a vacuum. It was … it was an awful sound. I could feel scraping, pain, and suction. I felt like a part of me was gone.

I was so ashamed. I felt … well, I couldn't even begin to explain my feelings at that very moment. I felt sorry and regretful for what I had just done. I wished I could turn back the clock. I felt worthless. I wasn't sure if I could ever face the world, my family, or my friends again. Even if they didn't know what I had just done, I knew. *I knew!*

I want to make it clear that I don't blame anyone except myself for what was done that day, not Mike or the father of my child, no one but myself. We all have to make our own final decisions, and I did just that. I can't change that fact. I wish I could. God knows I wish I could.

That was a horrible day that I will never forget. Then I heard the doctor say the procedure was over. The nurse told me to just lay there for a short time. They were walking back and forth in the room, rolling the tray away and out of the room. Then they took the machine that I considered was a suction or a vacuum. I laid there thinking to myself, *I just aborted my child! Lord, what did I do? I just aborted my child!*

The doctor and nurse were done, and it was time to leave the doctor's office. I got up off the table while the doctor and nurse talked with Mike. *I had no words to say.* I just got dressed and got ready to go home.

I wanted to go somewhere all by myself. Part of me wanted to go somewhere and talk with God, and yet the other part of me didn't want to show my face to God or anyone else. I knew I had made the biggest mistake of my whole life and that God would never, ever forgive me.

How could I ever forgive myself? What about my child? Could my child ever forgive me for cutting his life short? I didn't know what his life would have been like if he would have had the chance to live here on this earth. How could I ever face myself again? How could I face anyone? My heart wept deep down inside.

My heart wept

Mike waited for me, reached for my hand, and asked me how I was doing. I could tell he was happy and relieved at the same time that it was over. I'm sure it must have been different for him since he was not the one carrying the child and wasn't even the father. Maybe deep down it hurt him too. I never knew. We didn't really talk about it. We just left the doctor's office in silence. He had no idea how I was feeling. I didn't care to even talk about it or anything else. I felt that I had just left part of me in that room. I remember when they were done with the procedure, all I wanted to do was to get out of there. *I had just done the unspeakable, awful sin against God, myself, and my child. I was numb.*

The next day, I stayed in bed with cramps and pain, part of losing (aborting) the baby. All of the people who knew I was pregnant were told that I had a miscarriage. *What a lie! I'm a person who hates lies, and yet here I was telling a lie to cover up my mistake, my sin.* At this point in my life, I felt like life was just one big lie! I'd lied to cover Mike's drinking, about my life now with other men, and now about taking the life of my unborn child. These lies would haunt me for the rest of my life, and I felt I deserved that. My life was a mess. My life was so far from God.

One of my memories after having the abortion was when I arrived home from the doctor's office, my mother came to our house to see me as I lay in bed. I remember her asking me how I was doing.

My mother came to visit me

Keep in mind she thought I'd just had a miscarriage. I didn't tell her the truth until years later. She asked if she could do anything for me. I remember not knowing really what to say. I thought to myself, *This is my mother! How can I tell her I just aborted her grandchild? And yet if I don't tell her, then how can I keep this lie from her?* I remember her looking at me and wanting to help me with my pain. I couldn't look into her eyes. All I could think of was that I deserved every bit of pain that I was in. I felt it didn't compare to what I had done to my child and to my family. I told her thanks for being there and that it would just take time. I told her it would be all right. In my mind I knew it would never be all right. This would be with me the rest of my life. I had tears of sorrow. My mother saw tears of pain. *If she only knew that I had taken her grandchild's life. What would she say then? What would she think of me, her daughter? If I could only turn back time!* I had a lot of mixed emotions of anger, bitterness, tears, pain, and shame.

After going through an abortion, there are so many

painful feelings that seem to control a person. Here are just a few that I remember feeling.

- numb, like I couldn't seem to move, no feelings
- confused, disoriented
- hurt mentally
- fear, anxiety, dread
- betrayal, disloyal, dishonest to God, myself, and others
- unhappy, distressed, heartache, miserable
- shame, disgrace, irritated, self-disgust
- guilty, regretful, remorseful, sinful
- angry, annoyed

All I wanted to do was cry. I was not feeling sorry for myself but ashamed and regretful of what I had done.

In bed wondering why

After the abortion, I used to ask myself, *How can I go on?* I definitely felt that I couldn't talk to God. After all, why would He want to even hear my voice or hear my cries? I had committed this sin, this shame. I felt that I could never be forgiven, that I could never even ask for forgiveness. *Where was my sense of security? Was it in this world? In man? Or in God?* I found my security sure wasn't in myself, and obviously it wasn't in God. I felt my security was in man. That man was Mike and our marriage. I didn't want him to leave me. I wanted to please him. I wanted to keep our marriage. I can absolutely say that having the abortion didn't help my security in any way. It actually only made things worse. And it definitely didn't help our marriage. Things never changed between Mike and me. There were still problems with alcohol and no trust in our relationship. We ended up getting a divorce.

11

How Do I Move On?

The kids and I went one way, and Mike went another. I decided that I needed to go in and speak with someone in administration at the college. I felt like I couldn't finish school. My mind was so messed up that I couldn't think straight even if I wanted to. They were so good with me. I explained my situation with the divorce and my children and that I was looking for a place to live. I ended up taking a month off from my classes to get myself organized. (This helped me tremendously, but it also put me a month behind in all my classes.) At that time, we had an eviction notice from being behind on our rent, and we were also behind on all our bills. I had to find a place to live and figure out how I was going to try and finish school, get a job, and take care of and feed my children. I needed a job more than ever now, but I wasn't even finished with schooling. I didn't know what to do.

A friend from the college told me that the kids and I could move up to their place, which was about ten miles out of town, and I could help her by watching her two kids at night while she and her husband worked. This helped me tremendously, and I felt like I was helping her in some way. The biggest problem I had was my car breaking down a few times to and from the college. I remember one day I picked up my kids from the daycare and then picked up her kids. We were on our way to their house on the highway when we came to the dirt road that went to their house. I don't remember how far we had to walk on the dirt road. It seemed like it was a mile or so to their house from the paved road. My car broke down, so the four kids and I had to walk the rest of the way. I was taking turns carrying the smaller kids on the dirt road because their feet were hurting.

They had a doublewide mobile home that overlooked the valley and the Columbia River. It was so beautiful and peaceful up there. We had to be careful not to use too much water because the well was shared with their neighbors on the hill above their house. Sometimes when the well was low, the neighbors would use what little water was in it and left us with very little or no water at all. It was sometimes hard to predict how much water we might have for meals, laundry, and baths at night. It seemed challenging at times, but I was so thankful to have a place to live, and they were nice people to be around. My children were three and four years old now, and her children were just a couple of years older than mine, so they got along well. Mike had moved to his biological father's house, who lived about two hours away. Mike visited the kids once in a while. Life went on, and I realized that there was nothing I could do to change what had happened. I had to keep pressing forward.

During this time, my mind was such a mess. It was hard to concentrate on school. I was able to finish my schooling, and I earned my degree in accounting and data processing. I also was able to graduate with my class and was thankful that the college allowed me to go through the whole graduation ceremony with my classmates. They presented me with a blank piece of paper during graduation, and then after I finished the last month of my classes, I received the actual degree in my hands.

After graduating, I was so excited that I had all of my schooling behind me, and I was ready to get my resume out there and start a new job! I searched and searched and couldn't find anything. I kept getting letters from prospective employers saying I didn't have enough experience. I was really getting discouraged. I really needed to get a good-paying job to be able to support me and the kids. A friend told me about a job as a bar maid. I really didn't want that, but I figured it would be money coming in, so I took it. I worked one whole night and decided it was not what I wanted to do. I made great tips. In fact, one guy actually gave me a fifty-dollar tip. I made quite a bit in tips that night, but what a crazy job putting up with drunks all night. Men kept trying to get my number and grabbing me. The things those waitresses or barmaids had to put up with—crazy!

It gave me even more incentive to get out there and hunt for a decent job. I felt like the barmaid job was not what I had gone to school for, and I just needed to try harder to find the job I was looking for. I landed an office job working on the computer, basically doing data entry, answering phones, and helping with payroll. A woman there named Brenda trained me well. It was a Monday-through-Friday job with the hours of eight to five. This worked out great for the kids and me. It didn't pay as much as I would have liked, but it was a step in the right direction.

I was able to receive housing assistance, which gave me lower rent. With this housing program, I was able to pay rent, and the rent would increase as my pay would increase. It was such a tremendous help for me. We moved into a nice house right across from a school, and it was nice to take the kids to the playground there. It was a two-bedroom house and was perfect for us. One of the things missing, though, was a refrigerator, which I didn't have money to go out and buy, so I compromised. I picked up at very large Styrofoam shipping box that I would put my food in along with bags of ice to keep things cold. This seemed to work out fairly well, and I used it for about three months that way until one day when my ex-mother-in-law came over to visit. She saw what I was using and insisted that I'd use an extra refrigerator they had sitting in their basement. I was so thankful for it. I lived in that house for about six months when the landlords told me they had decided to sell the house and I would have to move.

I was so bummed and stressed. I started house hunting again. The thing was that I had to find a landlord who would accept the housing assistance program. Otherwise I couldn't afford the rent. I found a house that I was interested in, but it was a mess. It was so filthy inside and out, but it was in the same neighborhood and it was available. I didn't have money for a deposit, but I knew once I moved in there, I would still be able to use the housing assistance program until I got on my feet. I decided to ask the landlord if there was any way that I could move in and work off the deposit by cleaning up the place. He agreed. It was a lot of work, but it got my foot in the door and I was able to afford it.

12

Abuse and Relationships

I dated on and off for a while until I met a man I thought was fun to be around. He and I had a lot of fun together, and we did a lot with the kids. He was a part-time dad of his son, and he would see him once a month or so. His son was around the same age as my children. I made the mistake of getting involved with this man, and it ended in a really abusive relationship. He was a very jealous man. I would try and break it off with him, but he wouldn't take no for an answer. I couldn't believe I was going through this all over again—a different man in a whole different situation. I figured I had asked for it. Part of my reasoning was because I was scared of the whole situation and him not getting out of my life, so I'd just put up with it. A couple of times while I was at work, he broke into my house and was waiting for me in my living room when I opened the door. He would tell me that I would never be able to get rid of him. He put sugar in my radiator so it wouldn't run right so I couldn't go anywhere.

He would get drunk and lay in my front yard yelling my name, telling me he loved me and wanting me to open the door. The thing was that I would open the door and let him in just so he would stop making a scene in my front yard. This kind of stuff actually went on for almost a couple of years. I couldn't break away! One day I finally called the police because he told me if he couldn't have me, no one else would either. He threw me across my living room and against the fireplace. He went into my bedroom while telling me he was going to get my gun and shoot me. When he went down the hall, I ran down the street to a neighbor's house, who happened to be a police officer and also happened to be home at the time. Needless to say, the police came and arrested him, and I ended up getting a restraining order.

After going through all that, I didn't want anything to do with men in general. If and when I would go out, I would go with a bunch of friends. I didn't mind meeting a man somewhere for a date, but I'd go there and come home by myself with no attachments.

My husband now, Jack, worked hard to get me to go out with him after we first met. I actually met him through a friend while I was still involved in the abusive relationship. He asked if he could take me out for a date, and I told him I was involved with someone. About a year and a half or so later, Jack found out that I was no longer with the man, so he called and asked to take me out. What I knew of Jack I liked. At times we would talk for a while on the phone and he would want to get together, but I would tell him I was busy or that I couldn't make it for some reason or another. Sometimes I just didn't answer the phone because I just didn't want to have to tell him no. Like I said, I had had it with men by then. I wasn't about to go out with anyone at that point! I was afraid to get involved with anyone ever again. I felt that I had already gone through two very bad relationships (my marriage of eight years that was bad due to alcohol and the other relationship was due to abuse), so I just lost trust in men in general.

Well, Jack never gave up (and now I'm glad he didn't). Jack kept pursuing me until one day I decided I would go out with him. He was a gentleman. He treated me special, opened doors for me, treated me with respect, and always wanted my children around. The first time we went anywhere was when he asked if I wanted to go boating with him and some friends. I told him I wouldn't go unless the kids were allowed to go also. He said that would be great. We had a great time that day. Needless to say, Mitch and Castilia had a wonderful time boating also.

When I first met Jack, I remember him wearing Levi pants and cowboy boots—very handsome, I might add. His eyes are beautiful sky blue in color, and his heart is very warm. We dated for a bit, fell in love, and then decided to get married. Mitch and Castilia were eight and nine years old when we got married. I remember asking them what they thought about me marrying Jack. They were both excited and really liked him and wanted him to be part of our family also. Jack always wanted the kids to be involved whenever we did anything.

Jack and I have a lot in common in some ways, yet we are so opposite of each other in other ways. We both love the outdoors, boating, fishing, and camping, and now that we're older, we also love to go RVing. We both love family. He could never have children of his own due to medical reasons, but he loves kids. We both loved taking the kids with us, and at times their friends as well, on our outside adventures. We are opposite in the sense that I am a very social person and he is a very quiet and reserved person. We kind of balance each other out. Well, needless to say, we are still together after almost thirty years of marriage.

Mitch and Castilia's father, Mike, was still in their lives. Mike worked up in Alaska and would come down to visit with them about every three months or so. He would occasionally have a month or two off at a time. Mike and I continued to be friends throughout the years. Jack and I always tried to include Mike when the kids had special events going on in their lives. Both Mitch and Castilia finished school, got married, and had children. Mitch passed away about three years ago from pneumonia. He loved his children and his family very much. He had such a wonderful spirit about him. He always loved to laugh and joke. He loved working with his hands, making things, and fixing things. He went to college for welding and actually helped build a big stainless steel tree that has apples and pears cut out in it. It stands at an entrance of a small city called Cashmere, Washington. He was so proud of it. And of course, we were and still are proud of it. They did an awesome job. It's been hard the last few years without him here. I am looking forward to the day I see him again in heaven.

After Castilia graduated from high school, she went on to get her degree to become an art teacher. She has taught both junior high and high school students. She is very good at what she does. Students and other teachers alike really enjoy working with her. She is very creative and loves art. Art is just one area that she and I are alike. We both thoroughly enjoy it. We are also proud grandparents of seven grandchildren, two grandsons (Austin and Nico) and five granddaughters (Jade, Jewel, Mercedes, Tru, and Anya). I can truly say I love being a grandparent. It would be hard to imagine my life without them.

13

Telling My Secret

I kept the secret of my abortion for a long time. The only people who knew were my husband and my twin. It took me many years before I could even tell my mother what I had done. I was in my early thirties by this time. On that day, I sat down with both my parents and told them about the abortion. I remember it so clearly, going to their home and explaining to them that there was something important I needed to talk with them about and that I needed to talk with them with no interruptions. I told them it was something I had been wanting to tell them for such a very long time. When I told them about the abortion, I could see in their eyes that they were both very surprised and maybe even hurt. They didn't even know what to say or how to react at first, but they listened carefully.

They didn't say a word until I was finished. Then they talked to me about it. I remember I had tears in my eyes while I was talking with them. They didn't judge me or criticize me. They listened with open ears and open hearts. They were sad that it happened and wanted me to know they still loved me. My mother said that we are all human and that we all make mistakes in our lives. She also pointed out that in the Bible, Matthew 18:21–22 (NIV) says: "Then Peter came to

Jesus and asked, 'Lord, how many times shall I forgive my brother or sister who sins against me? Up to seven times?' Jesus answered, 'I tell you, not seven times, but seventy-seven times.'" I told her I had prayed and prayed about it and searched myself for answers.

I remember hearing about a book on the radio called *I'll Hold You in Heaven* by Jack W. Hayford. It is about healing and hope for parents who have lost a child through miscarriage, stillbirth, abortion, or early infant death. I ordered and read the book, and I would highly recommend it to anyone who has lost a child. I read how God forgives even me. It opened my eyes to so many things.

I had asked God to forgive me, but I also thought that I needed to forgive myself. Then I was told that if Jesus died on the cross and forgave me of my sins, who am I to try and forgive myself? There is no need to try and forgive myself because He has already forgiven me. Praise God! He has buried my sins in the sea of forgetfulness. The Bible also says in Micah 7:19, "You [God] will again have compassion on us; you will tread our sins underfoot and hurl all our iniquities into the depths of the sea."

I thank God that He is who He claims to be and that we can go to Him with any of our problems. He loves us with no conditions attached. No matter what we've done or where we've been, He's still there with an unconditional love that surpasses any of our understanding.

Asking for forgiveness

At one time in my life, I was too ashamed to go to God and ask for His forgiveness or even show my face. I was too ashamed to go to church. I even strayed further away from Him. The devil, the enemy of my soul, kept telling me over and over what a bad person I was and that I was already going backward, so I might as well just keep on slipping further and further away. But one day I really searched my heart and my life and where I was going in life. I looked to God and really sought His face and asked Him for forgiveness. He forgave me for not just some of my sins but *all* of my sins. What a sense of peace I received that day. He forgives. We just need to accept His forgiveness!

Now I feel it is time to tell others what happened in my life because I know that God has forgiven me. God has given me healing and hope. He showed me His mercy and His grace, and He wants me to share what He has done in my life.

If you or anyone you know has gone through an abortion or had anything to do with an abortion, whether you were the mother, the father, the doctor or nurse, a friend, or a family member, please know that God loves you. If you truly ask for forgiveness, you too can discover His forgiveness, His peace, His healing and hope. He is willing and able to give you all of these!

In God's plan, our aborted children's lives were not planned for an early departure from this earth. We made that decision for them. Even before we got to know them, their lives were gone. They had a purpose in life, but we ended that purpose early. Know that we will have a chance to see them again someday in heaven.

Psalm 139:13–16 (NIV) says: "For you created my inmost being; you knit me together in my mother's womb. I praise you because I am fearfully and wonderfully made; your works are wonderful, I know that full well. My frame was not hidden from you when I was made in the secret place, when I was woven together in the depths of the earth. Your eyes saw my unformed body; all the days ordained for me were written in your book before one of them came to be." This is such an eye-opening chapter in the Bible about the beginning of life and God's plan for our lives.

As stated in the *Washington Post* on September 30, 2015, The Guttmacher Institute's Abortion Survey stated that researchers found that the proportion of women expected to have an abortion by age forty-five decreased from 43 percent in 1992 to 30 percent in 2008. According to www.guttmacher. org in the March 2017 (Volume 49, Issue 1), there seemed to be a decline in abortions from 2008 through 2014 in the United States. In 2014, an estimated 926,200 abortions were performed in the United States. That is a lot of abortions! That is just in the United States! Statistics reported that 19 percent of pregnancies (excluding miscarriages) ended in abortion in 2014. Either way, it is a very high number. It's amazing the number of women who have had an abortion sometime in their lives. It could be your neighbor, your sister, your mother, a close friend, or maybe even you yourself. This is a subject that is just not talked about openly. It is held as a secret deep down inside of us, waiting to come out—a secret that we are scared to share with anyone.

So many men and women are hurting from making that decision to abort their child's life, some believing it was wrong and others who were uncertain. It is a very painful memory with lots of questions, pain, bitterness, and tears. I want to assure you that there is forgiveness and hope through Jesus Christ.

14

Will I See My Baby Again?

For the longest time I use to ask myself: *Will I ever see my baby again?* But now that I have made things right with God, I know I will see him again. I believe my child was a boy, a son. I named him Adam. I never had an ultrasound or anything to find out the sex of the baby. I just felt it in my heart. I still have questions like: *Will I recognize him in heaven? Was there a purpose? If God knows everything before it happens, then why … why did this happen?* Some of the answers to these questions I found in the Bible. Some answers I will not know until I meet my Maker in heaven.

What I went through definitely wasn't anything I wanted to share with anyone, especially my family, close friends, or even strangers. I realize now that God wants me to share this with others. Sometimes it is hard to talk about having an abortion and admit that I went through with it, but God said He would always be with me. Joshua 1:5 NIV says, "As I (God) was with Moses, so I will be with you; I will never leave you nor forsake you." I've always been told that God is no respecter of persons, so what He did for Moses, He can do for me and you. He'll be with each of us to the end if we ask Him to.

It's amazing when you think about how God put His Son on this earth to become one of us. Jesus went through all different kinds of trials and tribulations, yet He still died for our sins. John 3:16 (NIV) says, "For God so loved the world that he gave his one and only Son, that whoever believes in him shall not perish but have eternal life." He then ascended to heaven to later meet with us there. In the meantime, He did not leave us alone. He sent the Counselor, the Holy Spirit, to teach us all things. I believe the Holy Spirit was sent to comfort us, to guide us in our everyday lives. Even though Jesus died and rose again and ascended to heaven, He left the Holy Spirit to be with us here until we meet with Him someday in heaven. John 14:16 (NIV) says, "And I will ask the Father, and he will give you another advocate (Counselor) to help you and be with you forever." Isn't that exciting, knowing we are not alone no matter where we are on this earth?

For years I asked myself how I could have avoided going through with the abortion. Over and over in my mind I would ask, *Is there a way that I might prevent it from happening to others? What could I do or say? Would it really matter?* I prayed to God, *Please help me to help others. Help me to be a witness for You. Put me in a place that I might help others who are in the same shoes that I once was in.* I also prayed that God would give me the strength to witness for Him and tell my story for His glory alone and that I would put Him before myself in telling my story. He is the one who has given me strength to go on and the one I turn to in times of trouble. He is the only one who can truly forgive and forget. He reminds us of this in His word. Psalm 103:1-4 (NIV) says, "Praise the Lord, my soul; all my inmost being, praise his holy name. Praise the Lord, my soul, and forget not all his benefits—who forgives all your sins and heals all your diseases, who redeems your life from the pit and crowns you with love and compassion."

God has been working with me to tell my story for many years now. He's been speaking to my heart and letting me know that I need to help others that are in the same situation that I was once in. I wondered, *What can I say to those who are thinking of an abortion or trying to decide whether to keep their baby?* How could I say to them, "You'll regret it. Please don't do it. Think about what you're doing or stop and think about everyone who is involved and who all it will affect"? How could I give anyone advice about choosing life instead of an abortion when I have done this myself? Do I even have the right to say anything? I sure wished I had someone who would have taken the time to talk with me or that I would have taken the time to reach out to someone for advice (the right advice). Maybe then I would have really taken the time to think it out clearly and put my child's life above all other circumstances. Maybe I would have felt there was another answer. There were times when I felt like I should have no right to say that having an abortion is wrong to anyone. After all, I had been there, not only thinking and knowing that it was wrong but doing it anyway. There were also times when I wished I could have screamed just to get my point across.

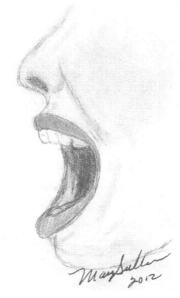

Feeling like screaming

But then I realized that yelling or screaming would probably only upset people and have the opposite effect on them. Although I would really love to say to them, "Please don't go through with it. It's probably not what you really want to do. Don't listen to what others have to say. Do what you feel is right. Listen to your heart, to God, and to the Holy Spirit within you!" I would also let them know that there are other choices that can be made.

God knows each one of our hearts. I believe we all have some kind of skeleton in our closet that we want to bury and forget. Maybe your skeleton isn't the same as mine? Only you know the answer to that question. Sometimes we need to let those skeletons out of the closet to be seen and heard. Doing this can be such a healing process for you or for others around you who may listen to your story. When things are hidden, it takes a toll on you physically, mentally, and spiritually. Don't let this happen to you. Know that your life is worth living!

There is a purpose, a fulfillment you'll never find anywhere else, which comes with such a peace, a calming, and a grace that only God can give as you lay your burdens down on Him. Let Him take those burdens from you. The Bible says in Psalm 68:19 (NIV), "Praise be to the Lord, to God our Savior, who daily bears our burdens." Matthew 11:28–30 (NIV) says: "Come to me, all you who are weary and burdened, and I will give you rest. Take my yoke upon you and learn from me, for I am gentle and humble in heart, and you will find rest for your souls. For my yoke is easy and my burden is light." John 8:36 (NIV) says: "He, whom the Lord has set free, is free indeed." And believe me when I say, from my experience alone, I can truly say a big amen to that!

He is waiting for you with open arms. Can you just picture Him holding you, telling you everything is going to be all right? I know I can.

Jesus holding me

Did you know that only you can be the one to turn your burdens over to Him? He will not take them from you unless you ask Him to. He died on the cross so He might forgive us of our sins (John 3:16). He did His part. All we need to do is ask Him and then receive it. It is truly that simple. Matthew 7:7–8 (NIV) says: "Ask and it will be given to you, seek and you will find; knock and the door will be opened to you. For everyone who asks receives; he who seeks finds, and to him who knocks, the door will be opened."

I have wondered how many others I could have helped in the past if I had opened up sooner with my story. How many can I help in the future? With God's help, I pray, many.

A lot has been said about how we grew up or what environment we were raised in seems to have an impact on us as we get older. I believe this is true, but I also believe that God gives us the strength and wisdom to get through it. Second Corinthians 5:17 (NIV) says: "Therefore if anyone is in Christ, the new creation has come: the old has gone, the new is here!"

I hope by writing this book that my story helps someone, anyone, whether it is from abuse or abortion or just being able to speak up when you know something is wrong. I had to give it to God to go on with my life. I had to push through the pain and the memories, and I pray that you can also. Don't cover it up, but face it head on.

Even in my earlier adult years, I felt that I should do what others thought was best for me. I was so naive. In reality, I should have done what I thought was right and walked away. Instead, I didn't, and I will regret it for the rest of my life. I blame only myself for my decisions. I had the final say regarding the abortion, but I did nothing about it. I was a coward to myself, my heart, and my God.

15

Asking God Why

With all my "should haves and regrets," I write this to you. God knows what is to happen to us before it even happens. We may sometimes ask "Why?" *If He knew I was going to go through with this, then why? What was the purpose of it? Why didn't He stop me? Why wasn't there any interference?* The only thing I can tell you is that He has given us the right to choose right from wrong. He does not force Himself on us. He is there for us, but we must choose to serve Him. Only He knows at this point the answers to the questions we ask. And maybe someday when we see Him face-to-face, we will receive those answers. But for now, we can only wonder.

Questioning God

God gives us wisdom that we must use. He gives us a choice to choose right from wrong. It's like a parent trying to discipline a child, letting the child know that if he or she touches the stove, the fire will burn him or her. Sometimes that child will still put his or her hand out and touch the fire or try to get as close as he or she can without getting burned. But once the child finds out that it burns and scars or feels that extreme heat, he or she is hesitant to make that same mistake again. As parents, we do not want them to even try, but sometimes they do it on their own anyway. Sometimes we just want to say, "I told you so," but all the while we still love them. It's a lot like us with God trying to teach us right from wrong. It's up to us to listen and choose right from wrong.

Have you ever noticed that when children have been burned or has a scratch or a scar, they show everyone? They also let everyone know what happened to them and how they got that scar or the burn. They might call it an "Oweee … ee" and tell you that they don't want it to ever happen again. Sometimes children will even tell a person how much it hurt to protect them or to warn them so they don't make the same mistake. We can be like little children at times and have to be warned. I am hoping to warn you by writing this book to you and/or to anyone who will listen.

The abortion is something I'm not proud of. I am so thankful that God is a God of second chances and that He has forgiven me. I can say with confidence that once I was ashamed but I am now forgiven.

God knows who my child is and what he could have done here on this earth if I had only given him the chance. I do know that I will see him again because the Bible promises me that. Unfortunately, I will miss the years here on this earth with him. I could have prevented this loss, and I will always regret my decision. I remember the day that I told my living children, Mitch and Castilia, that I had aborted a child, a sibling of theirs. I told my story to them separately, one on one. I explained to them that their mother took the life from this child. I waited to tell them about the abortion until I believed they were old enough to talk to. They both had children of their own by then.

Both of them were quiet at the beginning when I started telling them about the abortion. Their reaction was both of surprise and yet very caring. They both asked many questions. They were both very understanding. We've always had an unconditional love in our home. To this day I wonder what our lives would have been like with Adam and what kind of a person he would have turned out to be. I think about how many lives he could have touched.

A few years back, I spoke with a close friend about an unplanned pregnancy who had considered an abortion. I asked her not to go through with it and let her know it would be something that she would probably regret for the rest of her life. I told her about my experience and the regret I felt. I thank God that she did not have an abortion and that she kept her child. Years later she thanked me for talking with her. She is so thankful that she didn't abort her son.

I know that someday I will see Adam and that I will recognize him and he will recognize me. Praise God for His mercy and grace!

Seeing my baby again

God has given me the strength to go on. He has also given me the strength to talk about my past in hopes to help others. If you are going through a tough time in your life and you are contemplating an abortion, please think again. Really think it through before you make a decision. God loves you, and He loves that child too. God will always be there for you.

I wish I had been more informed about abortions at the time I had mine. I was told that the baby didn't develop until after three months in the womb. I now know, over thirty years later, that there is a child as soon as there is conception, an actual human being! And at that moment of conception, the baby has his or her own unique DNA. At six weeks, which is when I had my abortion, the baby was just starting to develop his brain. He already had all of his internal organs in various stages of development.

These are some of the things I learned after the fact: In the first trimester, the baby has the ability to suck his thumb, swallow, urinate, he can even make facial expressions. He can kick, turn, and make fists. He actually does all of his developing and begins to function in this first trimester. Did you know that the last six months of the pregnancy is only for growing and maturing? So if anyone tries to tell you that this child you are carrying is just "tissue" (this is what I was told by doctors in the '80s) or "it is not really a child yet," he or she is lying to you or doesn't know what he or she is talking about. It is a child from the beginning of conception, and an abortion does kill a child, a real, living human being.

Lifesitenews.com reports that scientific evidence shows that abortion is real and is a powerful trigger for breast cancer and that an abortion heightens a woman's risk of getting breast cancer. On August 18, 2015, Lifesitenews.com reported that researchers analyzing fifteen thousand deliveries have concluded that abortion creates a 30 percent greater likelihood of future pregnancy complications. Some women develop suicidal thoughts after aborting a child because of their regret and not being able to forgive themselves. Again on the Lifesitenews.com site regarding abortion and suicide, they reported that some psychologists have found in many post-abortion women common symptoms that include guilt, anxiety, depression, thoughts of suicide, drug or alcohol abuse, eating disorders, a desire to avoid children or pregnant women, and flashbacks to the abortion itself. Women who have already had an abortion have the right to know there is healing. If you or any women you know have any thoughts about having an abortion at all, you have the right to know the possible emotional risk associated with abortion. Please take the time to have an ultrasound. You'll be amazed to see the little person developing inside you even in the early stages of your pregnancy.

16

Finding Help and Forgiveness

If you previously participated in an abortion, whether you were the mother or father of that child, or maybe the parent or friend who took a woman to the clinic for an abortion, or anyone who had any part to do with the abortion, such as the doctors or nurses, I want you to know that God loves you and has the mercy and grace to forgive you. He can use you to help others who are facing the same circumstances and decisions in their lives. There are life-affirming clinics that need and could use your help. You might want to consider becoming a volunteer. A lot of times they can use help with administration, nursing, contributions, or even fundraising. Some people aren't able to physically help but might find that they can help out financially or maybe contribute by donating handmade baby blankets, clothing, or booties.

These pregnancy clinics give girls/women an opportunity to come in and discuss options for their child, whether it is to parent the child themselves or make an adoption plan. Most of these clinics give free exams and ultrasounds to pregnant girls/women, and they give the opportunity for you to talk with a doctor or a nurse. There are classes to teach the girls/women to care for themselves and their unborn child as well as how to care for the child after he/she is born. They will even include the father if he chooses to be involved. Some clinics give away items such as car seats, strollers, and baby items for finishing the classes. You can search for a clinic near you by searching for pro-life facilities on the internet. A place that I was associated with was called Life Choices or Real Choices. It is a Christian life-affirming ministry that provides medical pregnancy testing and educational services to women. They address women's physical, emotional, and spiritual needs.

They also hold classes for post-abortion women to find healing and restoration in a confidential environment. This group is called Post Abortion Support Sisters (PASS). This group really helped me through my post abortion issues, and I would highly recommend it to anyone going through the same issues.

God wants that unborn child to have the opportunity to live a physical and spiritual life. If you feel that you cannot raise the child on your own for some reason or another, make an adoption plan for the child. There are so many couples looking for the opportunity to love and cherish those moments with a child to call their own.

There is a couple I know who tried for many years to conceive a child. Nothing seemed to work. No doctors, medicines, or procedures seemed to help them. After years of trying and thousands of dollars spent, they decided to adopt. This was the best thing they could have ever done. Not only did they adopt one child, but a year or so later, they adopted a second child as well (which happened to be another boy from the same mother). Seeing them together as a family is so precious. You can see this joy and love has been extended to their grandparents, aunts, uncles, and other family members.

I have heard many stories from their grandparents of how these two boys have touched people's lives. I couldn't imagine what the parents' lives would have been like if they hadn't adopted the boys. Of course, the adoption has really touched the boys' lives as well. I attended a school function where one of the boys played three different instruments. Both boys are very talented. To know that these children were adopted in a loving home is more than words can say. But to also know that you have that choice to give life instead of taking a life can mean so many special moments to all those you and the baby's life will touch.

A few years back, I lost someone special. During his time in his mother's womb, he struggled to live. His mother found out that the baby had only one chamber to his heart instead of four chambers and only had one valve. This made his heart rate stay in the fifties. A normal baby's heart rate is between 120 to 160 beats per minute.

The first time I saw him was through an ultrasound. He kicked and moved like there was no tomorrow. He was only weeks old in his mother's womb. It was amazing to me to see how much of a little person he already was at that time. It made me smile. During the pregnancy, there were different doctors looking at him and trying to find out what was wrong with him. That's when they found the problems with his heart. The doctors suggested early in the pregnancy that his mother abort him, but she chose to give him the best chance she could, and she did.

The doctors talked about different medical procedures that could be done. These procedures included a pacemaker and/or a surgery to repair the heart (the chambers and the valves). They were to do this as soon as he was born. As time got closer to his birth, they talked about putting him on a pacemaker. They also said that when he turned two or three years of age, he would need a heart transplant to live. There just wasn't any other way. The whole time he was in the womb, he fought to survive. He lived just about seven months (twenty-five weeks) in the womb. She gave birth to him early in the pregnancy. He did not live. He actually died in her womb. I was able to hold him just after she gave birth to him. It was sad to know how much he struggled to live. His mother held him and wept at her loss (everyone's loss). He looked so peaceful as he went on to be with God.

As my mind went back in time, I remembered my past and how I threw away a life and how this baby boy struggled to survive. He is now in heaven with my child. He was here long enough to touch lives. I did not give my child a chance to touch anyone's life. I will have to live with that decision for the rest of my life. I hope and pray that no one else will make the same mistake I did.

On my knees

I pray that God's presence will always be with you. Let Him be your strength and guide throughout your pregnancy, from the beginning until the end. Place your trust in Him. He will guide you. The Bible says, "Children are a heritage from the Lord, offspring a reward from him" (Psalm 127:3 NIV).

Bible

It also tells us in Jeremiah 1:5 (NIV), "Before I formed you in the womb I knew you, before you were born I set you apart." God demonstrates His love for us that while we were still sinners, Christ died for us (Romans 5:8 NIV). Remember that any helplessness or hopelessness you may be feeling is from Satan himself. Surrender and humble yourself before the Lord. Don't withhold anything from Him. He will help you. We often take our confessions to God for forgiveness but not our guilt and shame. We need to give it all to Him. "Complete" forgiveness and restoration are ours through Jesus Christ.

I hope this short but painful journey of my life helps

someone in this world today. I hope and pray that even one life will be spared.

God is always there for you, even when you feel like you are all alone. Rely on Him. He can put someone in your life to help you through this journey so you are not going through it alone. He is full of love and forgiveness. He can give you a peace that you might have never thought was possible. He is there with open arms, full of grace, mercy, and love.

I ask that you listen to your heart. Talk with someone who appreciates life—someone who believes that God gives us this gift of life. We need to let the little children bless others with their lives, because life is so precious and sweet. Finally, may God bless you in every possible way. Remember that God forgives and forgets. All you need to do is ask Him. It's that simple.

I would like to explain to you how to ask God not only for forgiveness but also to ask Him into your heart for your eternal place in heaven: If you haven't done that before or would like to ask Him again, here are a few simple steps below along with a prayer to guide you.

His plan of salvation is for us to be born again. Have you ever wondered if you are going to heaven when you die? It is not a question of how good you are, or if you go to church, or how much money you give to charity. The Bible tells us that we must be born again. In John 3:3 it says, "Jesus replied, 'Very truly I tell you, no one can see the kingdom of God unless they are born again.'"

You might ask, "How can I be born again?" A born-again Christian is someone who has repented of his or her sins and turned to Christ for his or her salvation, and as a result we become part of God's family forever. God gives us His clear plan for being born again. *First, we must acknowledge God as the Creator.* "You are worthy, our Lord and God, to receive glory and honor and power, for you created all things, and by your will they were created and have their being" (Revelation 4:11).

Next, we must realize that we are sinners. "For all have sinned, and fall short of the glory of God" (Romans 3:23). Because we are sinners, we are condemned to death. This includes eternal separation from God. "For the wages of sin is death, but the gift of God is eternal life in Christ Jesus our Lord" (Romans 6:23). God loved each of us so much that He gave His only begotten Son, Jesus, to bear our sin and die in our place as it says in John 3:16. But God demonstrates His own love for us in this: while we were still sinners, Christ died for us (Romans 5:8). Although we cannot understand how, God said our sins were laid upon Jesus, and He died in our place.

God offers us the gift of forgiveness. You might say, "After all I've done, there is no way I deserve forgiveness." But guess what? God freely gives forgiveness! That's the point of grace. Jesus Christ took what we deserve on the cross for our sins and gave us a clean slate, a new beginning in life. No matter what we've done, God's grace covers every sin. Praise God!

In the Bible, a jailer asked his prisoners, Paul and Silas: "Sirs, what must I do to be saved?" They replied, *"Believe in the Lord Jesus, and you will be saved* —you and your household" (Acts 16:30–31).

It's very clear in the Bible that we believe in Jesus as the one who bore our sins, died and was buried, and whom God resurrected (just as we are taught and as we celebrate

Easter every year). It's Christ's blood and his resurrection that assures us of everlasting life when we call on Him as our Lord and Savior. "For everyone who calls on the name of the LORD shall be saved" (Romans 10:13). "Everyone" includes each and every one of us. So, if you understand that you are a sinner, and you believe that Jesus Christ came as the one and only Redeemer of sin, then you understand this plan of salvation.

The question is, are you ready to receive God's free gift of His Son, Jesus Christ? If so, here are the steps you need to take: (1) *believe in Christ*, (2) *repent of your sins*, and (3) *commit the rest of your life to Him as Lord by praying this prayer of salvation*:

> Dear God, thank You that You loved me so much, You sent Your Son, Jesus, to this earth to die on the cross for my salvation. I believe in my heart that You, God, raised Him from the dead. I ask you now to forgive me of all my sins. I will make Jesus Lord of my life. Help me to follow after You. According to Your word, I am now saved and will spend eternity with You. Thank You, Lord Jesus, for coming into my heart and for the help You will give me now as I trust in you. Please send Your Holy Spirit to help me obey You, and to do Your will for the rest of my life. In Jesus's name I pray, amen.

Congratulations! You have just been saved (born again). It is that simple.

The Bible says, "Repent and be baptized, every one of you, in the name of Jesus Christ for the forgiveness of your sins. And you will receive the gift of the Holy Spirit" (Acts 2:38).

As a new believer, remember to spend time with God each day. Read the Bible. Ask him to increase your knowledge and understanding of the Bible and your faith. Find a local church and friends to support you. Get baptized as Christ has commanded you.

One thing I would like to stress is that once you've given it over to God and you've asked Him to take it all away, you must believe it! Don't let the wounds of guilt weigh you down. Don't let your thoughts be open to Satan. He will just torture you over and over again with those sins of the past. Remember that God forgave you of those sins. You must believe in faith that He has taken those sins away. You're a changed person, a person who is free from those sins. You've already confessed your sins and turned away from the sin. Now believe you are forgiven in Jesus's name!

I welcome you to God's heavenly family. God loves you, and the angels are rejoicing and singing with Him above. You can now look forward to being reunited with your loved ones who are in heaven, even that child you may have aborted. God has forgiven you of all your sins and washed every one of them away. Perhaps by your healing, you will help others by sharing God's love and forgiveness regarding this delicate subject of abortion. God can give you the strength you never thought was possible. He did me.

17

Entries from My Journal

I would like to share some entries that I made in one of my journals about my abortion. One area was about my anger I had, and the other was a poem I wrote to my aborted child, Adam. I had so much anger that I held inside for so many years because of the abortion. I had anger toward myself as well as others. Here are some of the anger issues I had before giving them to God.

First: I was angry with myself for not being strong enough to stand up for what I believed in and how I was brought up and what I had been taught.

Second: I had anger toward the clinic, along with the doctors and the nurses that approved and performed my abortion, for not talking to me more about it, for not performing an ultrasound to show me there was life at that stage of my pregnancy, and for telling me that it was just tissue that I was aborting.

Third: I had anger within myself that I had no one to talk me out of it. The only people who knew were Mike and the father of the unborn child. I blamed myself for not reaching out and talking with anyone else about it.

Fourth: This one was really hard. I had anger toward God. I questioned God; if He knew everything before it happened, then why did He allow this abortion or any abortions to happen?

Then I prayed for God to open my heart and mind to confess the things I should, to forgive the people I needed to, and to do His will according to His word. I asked Him to heal my wounds and to forgive all who had anything to do with my abortion.

God knew my secret pain before I even knew it. I now totally trust Him. I thank Him for giving me the courage to talk to other women who have gone through an abortion and for stretching my mind through His Word to confront my past sins. Since my abortion, I have learned a lot about the growth of my child in my womb and his life. I had previously never really faced the anger I had inside toward the people involved in my abortion until now. I am blessed to know that God forgives even me. What a wonderful and awesome God we have!

I would like to share with you this poem that I wrote to my son Adam:

To My Son
God entrusted your life in mine,
A gift God uses to intertwine.
I didn't give you a chance to live.
I thank God that He does forgive.
I know He holds you in His arms,
From the time I caused you all that harm.
Because I wandered from God's grace,
I hid myself from His face.
I ask Him now for strength each day,
To show others abortion is not the way.

"Choose life" is what they must hear.
In their hearts, only to adhere.
I look forward to holding you again.
Please won't you forgive me of my sin?
Until we meet in our heavenly home,
A part of my heart will always be alone.
Love, Mom

I pray that each of you reading this book are willing to be open to God's wonderful mercy and love. May He bless you through and through, as He has me, through His grace and His power.

ABOUT THE AUTHOR

Mary Sullivan resides in Central Washington with her husband, Jack, and their shih tzu, Bella. They have a son, Mitch, who passed away from pneumonia three years ago and a daughter-in-law, Holly, who also lives in Central Washington. Their daughter Castilia and her husband, Juan, live in Florida. Mary and Jack are proud grandparents of seven grandchildren, two of whom are grandsons (Austin and Nico) and five granddaughters (Jade, Jewel, Mercedes, Tru, and Anya).

Mary enjoys being with family, camping, boating, and being around people in general. She also enjoys fishing and RVing with her husband. Her favorite pastime is painting. She loves to paint with acrylic and oil paint on canvas, tile, glass, and even rocks. She also enjoys teaching others her God-given talent of painting.

She didn't start painting until one day she woke up from a dream that she had of her mother. In this dream, she saw her mother in a beautiful garden in heaven. Mary had actually lost her mother to a brain aneurism a few weeks previous to this dream. The dream was so vivid to her with all the flowers and colors. She remembers that in her dream, her mother seemed so peaceful in God's garden. She knew she had to try to at least draw or paint what she saw in her dream. So she did just that. She then made copies of her painting and gave a copy to each one of her seven siblings. She has been painting ever since that day and either sells or gives her paintings away. She loves to see the smile on someone's face when she presents him or her with the gift that God has given her, her talents in the form of paint. Some of her drawings in this book go back about ten years or more. Her talent has improved since then, but she wanted to include some of her older drawings as they were part of her journey while writing her story.

Printed in the United States
By Bookmasters